North Berwick, the Bass Rock and its Gannets

Seascapes and Landscapes: Book One

Gannets feeding, east of the Bass Rock

Ian Goodall

North Berwick, the Bass Rock and its Gannets
Seascapes and Landscapes: Book One

Just a quick peck on the cheek, please

First published in Great Britain in 2014. This Edition published September 2017

Photographs taken on a Nikon D7000, D5200 or D5500
with a Nikkor 18-200, 18-300 or 10-24 lens

Bass Rock Books, 21 / EH39 4PZ, UK

BassRockBooks.com

ISBN-10: 1503223507
ISBN-13: 978-1503223509

About the author: Ian Goodall has been a photographer for more than fifty years. His photographs of nature, people, local events and news have been widely published in the press. Ian is a Council member of Edinburgh Photographic Society and Secretary of North Berwick Photographic Society

From the top of the Law looking north across North Berwick and the Firth of Forth

Introduction

Scotland has some wonderful scenery, the best usually associated with the Highlands and Islands. But less than 25 miles east of Edinburgh, on the Firth of Forth, the East Lothian town of North Berwick has its own magic and charm. It's so accessible by railway and road and is a gem of a place to live, to holiday in and to visit.

This collection of landscape and seascape photographs includes an amazing variety of coastline, countryside, beaches and islands from bays to the west and east of North Berwick harbour to, east of the town, Tantallon Castle, the Bass Rock and Seacliff. At the harbour visitors enjoy locally-caught lobster and take boat trips to the Bass Rock and May Island. This book includes photographs of huge waves pounding the coast, a high surge tide, spectacular sunsets, panoramas from the top of the Law, snow scenes and Christmas lights in the High Street. There's also a special 'up close' selection of gannets on the Bass Rock.

The Bass Rock is an iconic island. The plug of an extinct volcano it's home to the world's largest single-island gannet colony of over 150,000 birds. The Law, 613ft high with a whale's jawbone at the top, was also a volcano and provides spectacular views up the Forth Estuary towards Edinburgh and the bridges, across to Fife and beyond and the islands of Fidra, Lamb, Craigleith, May and the Bass Rock. East Lothian's rolling countryside and the Lammermuir Hills are to the south.

At North Berwick the weather, the light, land and sea magically combine to provide a photographer's dream. Enjoy!

Ian Goodall

PREVIOUS PAGES: Looking
west, north and east from
the top of the Law across
North Berwick. The whale's
jawbone is now a replica

ABOVE: Introduced in 2011 by the Moorland Mousie Trust,
seven Exmoor ponies graze on the Law. Beyond Broad Sands
beach, on the Firth of Forth, is the island of Fidra

This view from the Law shows the centre of North Berwick and the island of Craigleith. St Andrew Blackadder Church tower is on the left. Trees surround the Lodge Grounds, a well-maintained and popular public park with an aviary and children's play area. The park is a dog walkers' paradise

North Berwick visitors to the harbour are enjoying the fine summer weather. There's a queue at the Lobster Shack, on the right, which serves Jack Dale's locally-caught lobsters

Darkness was falling on 5th December 2013 when a high surge tide covered the Low Quay, causing some houses to be flooded. Described as "the biggest tidal surge since 1953", there was considerable flooding along the UK's east coast

North Berwick Rowing Club, founded in 2009, currently owns three skiffs, St Baldred, Skiff John B and Blackadder. Blackadder, on the day of her naming and launch, leads the way across North Berwick Bay

East Lothian Yacht Club (ELYC) is based at the harbour in North Berwick.
Regular races and training sessions are held throughout the season.
The club hosts international regattas and championships

Washed up. The Low Quay and the West beach with yachts from
North Berwick's East Lothian Yacht Club. A local fisherman's
boat is beached for some work to be done on the hull

North Berwick Bay and the West beach
on a delightful sunny autumn day

The anchor on Elcho Green with the sunset reflecting
off the buildings along the West beach

Braveheart, skippered by Dougie, has just
left the harbour with a party of fishermen

North Berwick's new lifeboat, Evelyn M, is piped down the West
beach after her naming ceremony in the Lifeboat Station.
A large crowd gathered for this special occasion

Launched from the West beach for their regular Sunday morning practice, North Berwick's inshore lifeboat is about to pass the old pier (out of the picture, to the right) which was substantially rebuilt in 2014

St Andrew's Church, on Kirk Ports, built in the mid-1600s, was abandoned and replaced by the 'new' church (with the Union Jack flying from its clock tower) in 1878

Viewed from the Lodge Grounds, North Berwick's
tennis courts host the annual East Lothian
Open Tennis Tournament

North Berwick Pipe Band performs at many local events and functions including the Raft Race and Lifeboat Day. In the summer, starting at 7.30pm every Wednesday, the band plays in the Lodge Grounds

North Berwick Highland Games are held at the Recreation Ground on the Dunbar Road every August. North Berwick Pipe Band leads the procession down to the town at the end of the games

The view across Milsey Bay towards the Scottish Seabird Centre
and harbour. The islands of Lamb and Fidra are beyond
with the Fife coastline in the distance

The island of Fidra viewed from Yellowcraig beach.
Fidra is believed to have been the inspiration for
Robert Louis Stevenson's "Treasure Island"

The 1st green of the par 70 East Links Golf Course has a commanding view of Milsey Bay.
The Glen Clubhouse, on the left, is a popular venue for social functions including
memorable Burns Suppers organised by North Berwick Drama Circle

Black Rock ('Yellow Craig') was a favourite 'hang out' of Robert Louis Stevenson.
RLS, who carved his initials in rocks further along this coast, spent summers
in North Berwick as a child in the 1860s with his family

This double rainbow went all the way across the Firth of Forth to the coast of Fife. Reflected in the water left behind by an outgoing tide on the East beach, the pot of gold was tantalisingly close

Perfect weather over Milsey Bay, out towards the Bass Rock and beyond to the North Sea. Dogs and their walkers on the East beach enjoy glorious early May sunshine and a mirror-calm sea. This photo was taken from the viewpoint on Castle Hill

PREVIOUS PAGES: Near Auldhame, looking north across a field of wheat towards Tantallon Castle and the Bass Rock

ABOVE: From the top of the cliffs at Seacliff there's a commanding westerly view to North Berwick Law, across to Tantallon Castle and beyond up the Firth of Forth

In a north-westerly direction, this view from the top of the cliffs at Seacliff takes in Tantallon Castle and the Bass Rock. In the distance the coast of Fife is just visible about 20 miles away

The massive curtain wall of Tantallon Castle, built in the 1300s.
The seige of 1651, ordered by Oliver Cromwell, left the castle
uninhabitable and it was never occupied again

Tantallon Castle is under threat again. Dale MacDougall-Haig, of the First Captain's Company, readies a canon for a 2014 re-enactment of General Monck's seige of 1651

The UK's smallest harbour is cut into the rocks at Seacliff. Car Beacon, near the end of the rocks centre-right in the picture, is at the mouth of the Firth of Forth. Beyond is the North Sea and Scandinavia

Seacliff harbour, where Jack's lobster fishing boat is moored. Lobster catches are good in these waters - perhaps not so good on the Fife side of the estuary as more East Neuk boats are appearing on the East Lothian side - and Jack holds up two lobsters from today's catch

Approaching the Bass Rock from the south on Fisher Lassie II from Dunbar. Landing on the Bass to see the gannets close-up is a 'bucket list' experience. Landing trips are exclusively arranged by the Scottish Seabird Centre in North Berwick

This view is from just over halfway up the Bass Rock, looking west. The island of Craigleith is straight ahead with Lamb on the left and Fidra on the right

These gannets don't have nests of their own but there are lots of nesting pairs nearby, many with small chicks

It's amazing how close to the gannets it's possible to get. A metre away is beyond the reach of a nesting gannet without leaving the egg or chick exposed to ever-present predatory seagulls

The gannet ("morus bassanus", named after the Bass) is the largest seabird in the North Atlantic with a wingspan of nearly two metres and a length of almost a metre

Mum and Dad guard their chick which has a full cover of fluffy
white feathers so it is probably about four weeks old

Landing on land is difficult for gannets even with plenty of space, as on this occasion. Crash landings in a very restricted area produce lots of noise and squabbles

Gannets feeding off the Bass Rock. Known as 'chumming', the boat crew throw whole fish over the side of their boat and gannets only need to do a shallow dive to catch a meal

PREVIOUS PAGE: View north west and north from the Law as the sun sets over Fife

ABOVE: The sun disappears behind clouds over Fife and it's dying rays just catch a dog being walked on the West beach

An amazing sky over Fidra, Lamb, Fife and the Lomond Hills. The lampost on the North Berwick harbour wall is next to the repaired collapse when the wall was nearly breached by heavy seas in 2012

Taming the Bass Rock. These waves were in December 2012,
when North Berwick's harbour wall was within one
row of stones from being breached

The same day as the previous photograph when a 40ft container, parked the day before in the harbour area, was tossed around by waves coming over the low seawall. It ended up in the harbour causing considerable damage. Several boats in the harbour and the boat park were wrecked

A snow-covered East beach viewed from Castle Hill.
Even the Bass Rock has snow lying on the top
(all the gannets are away at this time of year)

Christmas lights. Looking east along the High Street from outside the Golfers Rest public house. The Abbey Church Christmas tree lights and main High Street lights have just been switched on

The large anchor on a snow-covered Elcho Green frames the lifeboat station

Other books by the same author and available from local stockists and on Amazon:
"Glorious Gannets", "North Berwick, the Bass Rock and its Gannets: Book Two",
"From North Berwick with love" and *"Goodall's Guide to North Berwick"*

www.ingramcontent.com/pod-product-compliance
Lightning Source LLC
Chambersburg PA
CBHW041510280526
45792CB00004B/1200